Pease

and

Thank You!

"Lessons Learned
Growing Up
in
Small Town America"

D. StiRling Smith

Copyright 2007 – D. StiRling Smith / *StiRling Impressions*

DEDICATION

To my family whose profound impact on my life is immeasurable!

Walter (Buck) 1905-1973)
Ann 1907-1968)
Margaret (Peg) (1936-2004)
Elizabeth (Bette) (1938 -)
Sharon (1947 -)
Carol (1948 -)

To my Wife, Janie
and
my Grandson,
Marcus Stirling Smith
for continuing to provide me the inspiration
to move forward.

And to my beloved daughter
Rachel Janna Smith (1978-1997) who
Is in my thoughts and heart everyday.

Forward

I recently reached the sixty year milestone in my life. For many, sixty years old is no big deal, but for me, it was a major and emotionally eye-opening event for several reasons, which caused me to reflect on the early years of my life.

First, my Mom died when she was just sixty years old, so I have now outlived her.

Secondly, in June 2004, by the Grace of God and great medical care, I survived what should have been a fatal motorcycle accident. I have had three major surgeries in 2 ½ years. I now set off alarms at the airport due to there being more metal than muscle in my body.

Having spent six of twenty-four months in a wheel chair and another twelve in physical therapy, I've found myself (a former work-a-holic) forced into retirement. I now pursue professional photography and writing. Both of which I can accomplish within my limited physical capabilities.

I've had an abundant amount of time to reflect upon my life during these past three years. I've realized that I believe who we become as we mature, especially during those early formative years, is the result of God's grace coming into our lives through our daily relationships with our parents, siblings, family and friends, as well as our teachers.

This concept is certainly nothing new or profound. In these pages I've placed into print my own experiences as best I can remember them, growing up in Pease, Minnesota from my birth in 1946 to 1958, when our family moved to California. Those early years were among the happiest of my life.

I remain grateful for that innocent time, for my family, teachers, the church, and others that empowered and enabled me to have such a wonderful life. You taught me well.

As a result of the strong and loving foundation that was my upbringing, I have had a great and fulfilling career, traveled extensively, even met some famous and a few infamous individuals.

Since I've left Pease I've mourned the death of my parents Ann and Walt, my sister,

Margaret, and daughter Rachel, and rejoiced at the birth of my grandson, Marcus Stirling Smith. I've loved and lost, only to fall in love again, with Janie, the love of my life, and now my forever wife.

Through it all, standing alongside of me, has been my family and my God. All continue to be faithful to me and hopefully this little writing adventure will bear testament to their loving efforts which continue to this day.

Thanks Family – all of you!

2007
Spring Lake MI

Chapter 1

First Grade

Fall 1952. Not ancient history, almost not history. There was still a hint of summer in the air, and my young life as I knew it was about to be turned upside down. I began 1st grade at Pease Christian School in Pease, Minnesota.

There I was, leaving the safety of home, when my little sisters Sharon 5, and Carol 4, got to stay home with Mom because I had to go to school. It JUST wasn't fair! I couldn't remember ever being away from home in my life.

Facing Miss Strating was a daunting experience. Tall and slender, she was especially scary to a short, shy little six year old. I knew I would have to see her every school day for two whole years! I didn't even know what a year was!

Now, looking back, it wasn't so bad. The school did have running water in the hallway drinking fountain. But we also had an 8-hole boy's outhouse on the left side of a woodshed and there was an 8-hole girl's outhouse on the right side. There were four classrooms, 2 grades per room, totaling 8 grades in all.

Yep, Mom would walk me to school. Down those dusty unpaved dirt roads in our little Dutch immigrant, Christian Reformed town in North Central Minnesota, where my two older sisters, Margaret (10 years older) and Elizabeth (8 years older), had also faced the stern looking Miss Strating.

To top it off, I would have to eat lunch out of a bag! I had to walk there even though my Dad owned his own school bus! Life just wasn't fair! PERIOD!

I was only one of two "town boys", the other was my best friend, Don Godeke, and we were picked on by the "farm boys". Were we ever picked on! Now, Don was a bit more stoic than I was, or at least his fear of them wasn't quite as obvious as mine. I got "sick" almost every day for the first several weeks of first grade. I was allowed to walk back home, but when the screen door slammed behind me I realized I was not alone. Mom was there. So I didn't get to stay home for very long! She would give me a glass of milk or a cookie to reassure me, and send me back out the door to school.

Lesson Learned

I don't know how many times I tried that. But eventually I learned it's easier just to stay and tough it out. Get your assignments done. Whether it's at home, school, or work. Just do it! Thus, teaching me perseverance.

Thanks Mom, Dad, Miss Strating and others along life's way, for teaching me about dedication, commitment and hard work. It has made a tremendous difference in my life.

I was in the second grade when this photo was taken. I'm against the far wall - 2nd person back. Sister Sharon is the 3th person in the second row - cute blond.

Pease Christian School prior to 1956

Chapter 2

The Sand Pile

I remember the phone ringing, and listening with great anticipation as my Mom asked me if I wanted to ride with my Dad in the dump truck while he made a delivery. Driving a dump truck was his summer job, away from the noise and chatter of 50 or so kids on the bus while driving the rural dirt roads in Minnesota.

It had been some time since I'd gotten invited to go with Dad and I was wondering if it would ever happen again. We only had the school bus and Dad worked a lot of hours, so fishing, hunting, and all that other stuff just didn't happen because he was always too busy. But occasionally I could go to work with him and that was cool, real cool! Getting to ride in a real dump truck and even pulling the levers and all that other "man stuff" was exciting. But more importantly, I could spend one-on-one time with my Dad.

In those innocent days a boy could be sent down the road alone to wait for his Dad. It was probably just as dangerous then as it is now, but we just didn't think about it. So, I was sent down those same dusty roads that I walked to and from school on to Highway l69, one of the main highways right through the middle of the state. I was seven or eight years old, just standing along the side of the highway waiting for Dad and his dump truck.

There he'd come, blowing the horn, pulling to a stop and then off we'd go. If I was really lucky, he'd stop at a coffee shop for pie and ice cream; I'd have a Coke-a-Cola and he'd drink the cream straight out of the miniature milk bottle that came with his coffee so as not to have it go to waste, even though he didn't take cream IN is coffee. Waste not, want not.

Thanks for the miniature milk bottle – Sharon

It was a grand adventure for me! Perhaps we would go to Princeton, or St. Cloud, or maybe, if I WAS lucky, it would be to Minneapolis/St. Paul and we'd see the Mississippi River. Best of all, I could tease my sisters about seeing something they hadn't seen when I got back home. For Dad it may have been just another day at work, but I'd like to think he wanted to spend some quality time with his only son.

Then one day there had been no call. The dump truck just came rumbling up the road! Noisy brakes, double clutches, downshifts and finally it turned into the driveway. Yes! Yes! Dad was coming to get me, and rescue me from the sisters and their "nonsense"! But... wait... he stopped, turned the truck around, backed up, pulled the levers, and VOILA! Out came an instant sand box! Minus the box. He had dumped about 5 yards of raw wet sand, tree roots and all, into the yard. Mom glared, Dad smiled, waved, and said, "have fun! See you kids tonight!" I think he came home late to a cold dinner.

Lesson Learned

It's not how much time or how much money we spend on each other or our families that matters. Sometimes it is just the simple things that matter most. Like delivering a BIG pile of wet, dirty sand in the yard for kids to play in. Dad was a hero to us that day. Caution...Mom may not think so. Even 50 years later, Dad is still my hero when I remember that one special day. I'm tempted to go see if the soil is still sandy in that spot. I hope it is.

Chapter 3

The 4th of July

Just before dawn, somewhere outside of the Pease picnic grounds, back by the big hill near the cemetery, some of the town "elders" always started the day's festivities with the traditional explosion of a few sticks of dynamite. My father would never tell who, exactly, ignited the explosion. State secret, I suppose.

Mom was more interested in making sure that whichever of us kids was in the flag drill that year was properly groomed, and that the triangular cape was appropriately starched. The alarm was set so we could all make it to the church on time.

The 4th is more than just a holiday in Pease. It is a week long family reunion. There's food, fellowship and laughter. That's why the picnic grounds are next to the cemetery, it's a family reunion for the living AND the dead. Though they never ate much.

The celebration started at the church, then moved to the picnic grounds. It really was a community picnic, with food like boiled hot dogs, games for the kids, three legged races, pillow fights while straddling a greased pole, cap guns, searching for coins in the huge pile of sawdust which would be revisited for days afterwards. Sending tin cans high into the air with firecrackers, much to the dismay of moms and the encouragement from fathers.

I remember the sulfur-like smell of gunpowder from roll after roll in the cap guns. But the guns were never, never to be pointed at anyone, even in jest. Just ask my sisters, they still won't tell me where they hid mine. A few of them have probably turned to rust in the branches of some of the trees on the picnic grounds.

Then, the world's greatest fireworks! All in all, it was purely a display of open, heart-felt, honest and sincere small-town American patriotism. Oh! What a day! How a town of 165 citizens could put together an Independence Day celebration complete with a display of fireworks that continues to attract thousands each year.   Amazing! Amazing! Hats off to you!

Flag Drill Participants mid 1940's. Sisters Bette and Margaret (1st and 2nd from left, front row)

Lesson Learned

It's OK to wave the flag! Remember, it's our God given freedom to spend time with our families, play games, reminisce, pray, enjoy fireworks, say OOOH! and AAHH!, feed the mosquitoes, and to be patriotic, singing the "Star Spangled Banner" while standing at attention. That is also where I learned to love the "Battle Hymn of the Republic". I've asked that it be sung at my funeral, because I love it so much.

Chapter 4

The Big Hill

Like most kids in the upper Midwest, by Thanksgiving weekend the Smith kids were anxiously awaiting the first snow, for several reasons.

The first was that maybe my Dad, the school bus driver, would give us a ride to school in the bus rather than make us walk. Or maybe the school superintendent in Milaca Public schools would call Dad and ask him the condition of the roads "out there" and school would be cancelled. The second was if school was cancelled we wouldn't have to wait until Saturday to go to the "Big Hill" to go sledding.

After warm oatmeal, and weekly chore completion in preparation for Sunday, we dressed warmly for the day's outing. We layered. We just didn't know it as the term "layering" is used today. We simply put on a lot of clothes. Long johns, a flannel shirt or two, two pair of pants (or, as sister Carol says in her "Pease Speak", Pantses).

A sweater or two, then a coat, scarf, cap or hat and either knit mittens or brown Jersey work gloves.

Now, you had to have at least two or three pair on, plus one in your pocket, and one at home on the register warming. We should have had stock in the jersey glove company.

Off we would go. First we'd call Don Godeke to meet us at the cemetery because you had to cross the cemetery to get to the "Big Hill. Carol, Sharon, Don and I would make our way over the graves, through the rusty barbed wire, ignoring the "No Trespassing" signs, dragging our sleds, cardboard boxes, flying saucers, toboggans, and whatever would make it down the hill the fastest. Sometimes it felt like we were the only kids in town until we went to the "Big Hill", it was the place to be!

Up and down, up and down, we crashed into each other, over each other, over the "jump", and through the trees. Rolling the sleds, sometimes breaking them. Even occasional blood letting was not unusual, and this would just be the morning round of sledding. We had no watches. We watched the sun, and usually made it home just in time for hot Campbell's Chicken Noodle Soup and crackers.

Then a change of gloves, and a change of wet outer pants (pantses), and back to the " BIG HILL".

Around 3:00 pm, when the Northwest prairie wind came up, our inner clock, or actually, our numb feet and our frozen hands, (those jersey gloves and mittens weren't waterproof) told us it was time to head home.

Then came the best part of the day! I can still smell them! Warm, homemade cinnamon rolls with raisins and lots of brown sugar turned to caramel and smothered with John Godeke's (the local butter maker, and Don's father) rich creamery butter and hot tea. That made the whole day worth living. The memory still makes my mouth water.

Lesson Learned

Life is ups and downs. Sometimes the ride down is a whole lot of fun and extremely exhilarating and scary. There is nothing like that feeling. But then, at other times, there may be some hot tea waiting for you and the wonderfull smell of homemade cinnamon rolls with raisins and the feeling you get is even better than the "rush" of zooming downhill at a high rate of speed. Life is good, no matter what.

Go ahead. Find your Mom's recipe for one of your childhood favorites and try it yourself. I did, and I am glad. They weren't as perfect as Mom's, but the memories were.

Cinnamon Sweet Roll Recipe

Anna Hubers Smith

3 c. warm water
3 tsp salt
½ c. sugar
½ c. shortening
2 eggs well beaten

2 packages of yeast in ½ c. warm water and 1 tsp sugar. Combine above ingredients and add flour gradually, stir until all ingredients are thoroughly mixed.

Try 9-10 c. flour until you achieve the right consistency. Knead well approximately 15-20 minutes.

Let rise in warm area (without drafts) until it rises over the top of the pan. Use a very large bowl (the largest Tupperware bowl works well) or a large stock pot to mix ingredients. Punch down and let it rise again.

For cinnamon rolls, break off (1/5) portion of raised dough and roll out on floured surface with rolling pin. When about ¼ - ½ inch thick, spread with melted butter, cover with brown sugar, raisins, and cinnamon and roll all that up into a long roll.

Then cut into pieces about 1 ½ inches thick and place in pan (Pyrex round or square) which you have prepared with melted butter and brown sugar (coating the bottom to make a caramel topping).

Makes about 4 dozen cinnamon rolls. Bake @ 325 for 30-35 min.

Chapter 5

The Bus

It was really embarrassing! "Here come the Smiths' again"...in the bus. We didn't have a car, we had a bus. A real big 1947, 6 cylinder, 3 speed, 48 passenger bus, complete with the smells of sweeping compound, rotten apples, stale sandwiches and farm kids sweat (ie: manure). Why, oh why, couldn't we have a car?

Imagine this, we are going to the big city of St. Cloud, thirty miles away. Dad, with his driving hat, driving of course. Mom in the right hand seat, Bette and Margaret a few seats behind her, the younger girls behind them, and myself, as the "heir apparent", in the seat of honor behind Dad. Looking over his shoulder, watching every move he made. Noticing how fast he was going when he shifted from first to second and finally to third. Asking a myriad of questions. Unable to contain my curiosity about why certain vehicles were the way they were, and letting him know that I knew most of the makes of the cars coming at us.

Since there was no radio in the bus, Mom would insist that we sing hymns. It was like double jeopardy. Usually we would go to town on Saturday, because we would have to go to church the next day. So this was a warm up. Sing our way to St. Cloud. It was embarrassing enough to have to go there in a bus, drive around looking for a parking place, and then to have to sing hymns all the while besides. Enough already! However we did get a very short reprieve from the hymns by singing "London Bridge is Falling Down" as we drove over the Mississippi River.

Visiting relatives, even near-by relatives, was equally embarrassing. They could see us coming down the dirt roads for miles. So much for drop in surprise visits. Sometimes though, just for fun, Dad would take us real fast over a hill so we would fly out of our seats. Bear in mind these were on bumpy dirt roads. We never hit anything except maybe our heads. Miracle?

The Bus also served not only as a summer play ground, but as the Smith version of an RV. Yep...just unbolt a few seats, turn them around, add some boards, grab some homemade handcrafted quilts, pillows, canned food, firewood (no briquettes back then), marshmallows, and some blankets to be used as privacy curtains and the Smith RV was ready to roll. Oops, I almost forgot the Chamber Pot wedged into a secure corner where it couldn't tip over.

Lesson Learned

Life's embarrassments are usually just of our own perceptions. When I turned 60 I found out we were the envy of Don Godeke because we had the bus and all they had was a gray Hudson. For Don, riding in the bus was an adventure, especially when their family joined us. Thanks Don, for clearing up my own misconceptions!

Chapter 6

Remember the Sabbath

Our last few years in Pease we lived next door to the Pease Christian Reformed Church, the church Parsonage, and the town store. We were at the heart of the town, so if anything happened we knew about it. Pease was a busy place six days a week, but on Sundays (the first day of the week) it was especially busy. On the first day of the week we honored the Sabbath. We were scrubbed clean the night before (the weekly bath).

Boy! Did we remember the Sabbath! Divine Worship twice, where the preacher (AKA the Dominie) PREACHED AND PREACHED AND PREACHED. The elders and deacons sat separate from their families, looking dour. We dreaded it, except for the long prayer peppermint break. It was kind of like half time or intermission where we reached into Dad's pocket for a peppermint and, if we were fortunate, got the pink one.

Then, afterwards, Sunday School. Then always to coffee at some Aunt or Uncle's house, traveled to in the big yellow bus. Once there, we had to sit in our Sunday best, behaving our Sunday best, with sore feet because of having to wear our Sunday shoes. Was this Protestant penance?

Then home for either chuck roast or a roast chicken and boiled potatoes with gravy. Thank goodness for gravy on Sunday, I think it helped the sermon stay down. Potatoes had been peeled, corn, beans, peas, etc., had all been partially prepared the night before in honor of the Sabbath.

Of course, after the meal, there was the obligatory Sunday afternoon "nap" for Mom and Dad. I still believe one half of the Christian Reformed Church children were conceived on Saturday night after the weekly bath and the other half during the Sunday afternoon "nap" while us kids studied our Sunday school lesson in advance for the next week, as we had to be prepared. Remember: "everything done decently and in good order".

Prior to evening worship, we were allowed some time to vent a little energy. But it was like NASCAR restrictor plate racing, nothing to excess. We could play catch, but couldn't play ball (no bats allowed). We could go for walks, but couldn't run races or ride bikes. We could draw, but quietly, so as not to disturb Mom and Dad's "nap". Get the picture? For us kids, it was a bit prohibitive.

Lesson Learned

OK, so maybe it was a little too much. I still have a bit of hesitation on what Sunday activities (not "naps", I'm not that conservative) should and shouldn't be. Sunday is a day of rest, intended for our bodies as well as our souls to re-energize. But maybe we should make sure to keep it the Lord's Day. Not just a day for fun and relaxation, but a day for worship and the praising of our Lord.

Pease Christian Reformed Church Late 1950's

Chapter 7

Television, a Fix-It Shop and a Spanking

In the early days of television most of us kids gathered at Mr. Roelof's Shoe Repair and Fix-It Shop next to the Pease Post Office, across the street from Baas' Garage. It was a wonderful, dark, damp, dank, dreary, smelly place. With piles of shoes, small appliances, rubber cement, solder, burnt electrical tape and more stuff than a kid's mind and senses could ever grasp. Between Mr. Roelof's pipe smoke and the burning coal embers in the stove, it's a wonder most of us even survived to adulthood.

But to us, because there was no parental supervision for those few hours, it was a taste of freedom. Like the kind of freedom that respectable adults like my Dad and the area farmers had when they gathered at the Pool Room Annex of the café on Saturday mornings to shoot pool. WHY? Just because they wanted to.

So, there we were. Sharon, Carol, Don, Randy his older brother, Mary and a few other town kids all huddled around that little black and white TV in the corner of the Shoe Shop after school. Completely fixated on the shows that we thought would expand our minds from the past and into the future. There was Hop-a-long Cassidy, Roy Rogers and Dale Evans, cartoons, and Superman. Hour after hour after hour we sat, mesmerized.

Our Mom, thought it was just plain awful! "My, My", what would become of us? Would we become TV addicts without a future, without hope, without a work ethic? Were we exposed to violence, wanton waste of life, endless mindless chatter? I really don't remember much of what we watched, but I do remember how magical it felt to be transported back in time or forward in time as Flash Gordon explored other worlds. However, one fatal day I remember going there against my Mom's wishes and getting caught.

Even "Butch", everybody's favorite, wasn't above the law. Dad would have to deal with me when he got home! Of course, he came home late that day and the time spent waiting made it even worse. It was the only spanking I remember my Dad ever giving me. I still don't believe he wanted to do it.

After all, he was raised a Methodist, and they didn't have as many rules that required a spanking as Mom's Christian Reformed ones did. I think it hurt him as much as it hurt me. In truth it probably hurt him more because I faked a lot of screaming. Hey it worked at the time!

Lesson Learned

Honor your Mother...regardless! Remember, she wrote the rules and convinced Dad to enforce them (smart man for doing so). Just make sure the punishment fits the crime before the sentence is doled out. I would have a "perfect record" except for that one spanking.

Chapter 8

My Dog Corky

I'm not sure of the actual year, but sometime in the mid 50's, Don Godeke had "Bootsie", his happy, glandular challenged, rotund, playful, temperamental dog. And after having a series of cats that had received their eternal reward, we got my dog, Corky.

Note I wrote that we got "MY" dog. It was my whining, complaining, temper-tantrum throwing, and whatever else it took to persuade Mom and Dad we ("I") needed a dog that they could no longer stand. So when Rev. Bult's family next door got "Taffy", a female cocker mix, we got a male cocker from the same litter and I was ecstatic! I had "our" dog, Corky.

We bonded and we bounded. Except for church and school everywhere I went Corky went. To bed, to play, to the bathroom, to the Fix-It-Shop, to Kiel's Hardware Store, to Baas' Garage, to play in the swamp behind the picnic grounds...we were inseparable.

My energetic, hyper-friendly dog even bonded with my clothes, it seems. When Mom was doing laundry in the basement Corky would sort through the clothes and find my socks and take them outside or back upstairs and hide them under my bed.

He would ignore other family members and respond only to me. He provided protection too, even to the point of biting Donnie and earning a two week rabies grounding on the clothesline leash. His clothesline quarantine was just a parental safeguard, as we didn't go to doctors for much in those days. He also protected us from the "dangerous" cows in Moorlag's pasture behind Don's parents house, earning him another grounding to the clothesline.

I'll never forget the day Dad told me he sold my dog to a truck driver passing through town. I didn't know at the time that we were getting ready to move to California and Corky couldn't come with us. It was a very sad day for me.

Lesson Learned

Every young boy needs a dog and inside of most men are fond remembrances of their childhood dog even if some of the memories are sad, and that's OK...in fact, that's GREAT!

I hope you believe me. As I can attest to the fact that pets help provide healing for the loneliness of the heart, the discouraged soul, and the broken body. I even got a few tears in my eyes as I wrote this, when our wonderful collie, "Juliet" nudged me to give her a little scratch behind the ears.

Chapter 9

"Grace"

My Mom was perhaps the most wonderful Mom there ever was. I'm sure a lot of boys and men say that. Unfortunately, she died much too young. But the impact of her life continues to live on in our family more than we realize. I am blessed to see that the promises of scripture continue to be true, as her memory is honored by her children, grandchildren, and great-grandchildren from generation unto generation.

I've been fortunate to have been "adopted" by many other "moms". Like my four sisters; Margaret, Bette, Sharon and Carol. Even though I'm into my 60's, they continue to "mother" me. I really do enjoy being their only brother and I am spoiled rotten! (just as they accuse me of being).

Another "mother" was Grace Godeke, Don's mother. Since Don and I were only 3 weeks apart in age we spent a lot of time together growing up. And since I had more sisters from whom I needed to escape from and his older sister, Garda, was cuter than my sisters, even though there were really kind of cute, I spent a lot of time at his house. I felt like part of the family. We were like brothers. We were punished together, potty trained together and I even was banned from playing at his house for a time, until I learned to "pee straight" (a lifelong problem according to my wife).

One particularly warm summer day I decided to make up a little ditty about "mother Grace" which wasn't too nice; especially for a 9 year boy to say about his friend's Mom. Needless to say, I was caught, and had to make "THE WALK" across the church parking lot, head hanging WAY down, to apologize to "mom Grace". How I wished that lot had been five times bigger, because it was the world's shortest, loneliest walk. I stammered out "I'm sorry" and Grace responded with... well... with grace. "Go play"! And that was it!

Lesson Learned

About thirty five years later, while on a business trip in Minneapolis I visited withJohn and Grace. I drove up un-announced, knocked on the front door (brave, huh?-you never went to the front door) and when Grace opened it, asked if I still had to take my shoes off at the door.

She responded with "Well I'll be! Oh my! Come on in "Butch"! GRACE knows no expiration date, and sometimes we don't even know when it begins. My "other mother", Grace, taught me a wonderful lesson. I didn't even realize that until a few years ago. Thanks for the wonderful lesson in grace, "Mom" Godeke.

Chapter 10

My Dad's More Important
Than Your Dad
OH YEAH!

I have never quite figured out how two best friends could argue so much. I mean siblings I understand, but best friends, I don't.

Don was usually the General or at least a Major. I was always the Sergeant (I actually became one later in life). He was the sheriff, I was the outlaw, but I always escaped his jail.

When it came to building roads in the sand-pile, mine were the super highways. His were the quiet side streets with the fancy houses, as he had help from my sisters. Then the flood would come and the river would overflow the dam that I had built and wipe out his town. We would argue about it and he would go home for an hour or two or till the next morning. It seems quite silly now, but back then we cared that we hurt each others feelings, so we would make up.

One thing we never did settle was whose Dad was the most important. My Dad was the bus driver and made sure the kids got to school safe. His Dad was the award-winning National Champion Butter Maker who had met President Truman, and was the Mayor of Pease.

But in my mind my Dad did this, so he was the most important, in his mind his Dad did that, so he was the most important, and that was the way it was going to be! Both of them worked hard to put food on the table and when I look around at both of our families I think we all turned out pretty darn good.

We have all had good lives, careers, and families. We are reasonably healthy, successful and none of us have spent any time in jail (at least that I know of) and we all worship the One True Living God.

Lesson Learned

What was so wrong with arguing about who's Dad was the best? We both loved our Dads a lot and still honor their memory and that's how it should be. Honoring your Father and your Mother is OK!

Chapter 11

The Museum

I guess Sharon, Carol, Don and I must have been bored one day. Either that, or Mom was just tired of our badgering and pestering each other. So we were banished to the garage to clean it up.

First of all, there was the dog house in the corner that had to be dragged out. I still think it was made out of the world's heaviest oak, or something that would have supported the front end of the school bus during an oil change. Then all the other stuff, the push lawn mower, Dad's and my late Grandpa Smith's tools, rusty paint cans, extra bus tires, winter snow tires, extra wheels, a trailer hitch (we didn't even have a trailer), racks, shovels, lumber, the storm windows, and even a live bat or two, along with some field mice.

That must have been the easy stuff that took us most of the morning. We found more stuff that afternoon which stimulated us to create the "museum project". Why not have a museum? We could have a gate, charge admission, sell kool-aid, and on and on it went. By 4:00 pm the garage was cleaned out, and we began in earnest to organize our "museum".

I was to invent the gate and collect admission. Sharon, Carol, and Don would gather the exhibits and organize them. As we quickly ran out of exhibits, a "scavenger hunt" was necessary.

Laurence Kiel allowed us to explore the basement of the hardware store for treasures like "gold" shirt buttons, at least that's what we advertised them as, some old tools, and bottles, etc.

We then had a viable museum, along with a gate, a restaurant area, and a waiting area which was needed, 'cause the lines were going to be long. We even had signage for the store part because we were convinced we going to make enough to, well, maybe go to the Ben Franklin store in Milaca, all of 4 miles away and buy something.

You know what? We did have customers, and even though amused, they were considerate enough not to laugh. Laurence Kiel came with someone and even paid the full fare, bought kool-aid, and patiently waited three minutes to get in.

We were a success! We had a relatively long waiting line, sold out on kool-aid, (I think Carol drank it most of it), and the gate didn't break. Nothing fell on anyone and everyone had a good laugh at our "chamber pot" labeled "old fashioned cooking pot"

Lesson Learned

Dreams and youthful entrepreneurship often come true in many ways down the road. Through my military service, five years in restaurant management, and thirty years in the Christian Media Ministry that same inquisitive, inventive spirit was drawn upon time and time again. At one point I was told I was the "master scrounge", and at another I was given the title of "the answer man", I accepted both as compliments.

I just made sure that I always knew the difference between a chamber pot and a cooking pot before putting a label on it.

Chapter 12

Tools

In my garage and basement are the "tools of the trade" that my parents used. One of them is my mother's Mix Master, circa 1950 and it still works just fine. It's been moved from Minnesota to California, to Michigan and somehow it ended up with me. Even with "encouragement" from my spouse I just don't have the heart to throw it out.

To me, it's a symbol of a simpler life. Of a Mom who put her heart and soul into home itself as well as homemade cakes, cookies, and soups. I remember moving the level to the side and when she wasn't looking, sneaking my finger in to get a quick taste of whatever she was making…ummm….good!

In the garage is a box of rusty tools, gathered by my father with his uncanny ability to spot a screwdriver or wrench in the middle of the road while doing 60 miles an hour in the bus. Whenever he brought home a "new" mechanic wrench or carpentry tool most were already very well used by the time he got them. They became even more used by the time I inherited them from him. But they were more than adequate to help him make a living, and keep our homes and vehicles in reasonable and functional repair.

One of my most prized possessions is a small hand-forged tack hammer passed on from my rural mail-carrier Grandfather, Samuel Jesse Smith, to my Dad, to me. It will someday be passed on to my grandson, Marcus. It is like the "Holy Grail" in the family, to be touched, but never used, only admired. It symbolizes our heritage of humble beginnings, hard work and family.

Lesson Learned

To me, that little tack hammer reveals family values; heritage, history and our future. But just remembering our past really isn't enough to guarantee us a future. We need to honor those who went before us by continuing their legacy. Not just by providing for our families, but by using the tools we each have been given to serve each other , our families, our communities, our churches, our country, and our God.

Chapter 13

Hands I

I remember, as a child, looking at hands.
A few of them really stand out in my mind .
Uncle Stan's were a lumberman's hands,
Uncle Rudolph's, a farmer's hands. My Mom
and Dad's hands I remember vividly.

Mom had fine, narrow hands with transparent
skin that you could almost see through. You
know the kind...shine a flashlight behind them
and you can see the veins, tendons, and
bones. On her left hand was a well-worn
wedding ring. warped , quite often from
being run through the ringer washing
machine. She never wore any other jewelry
on her hands. Just that one simple ring for
those elegant but simple working hands.

Those were the hands that raised five kids.
Three of us came along one soon after the
other, in two and one-half years. Remember,
no running water, no disposable diapers, no
prepared baby food.

Those hands also washed windows, sewed
clothes, darned socks, cooked meals, and
volunteered at school. But no matter what,
those hands were always available to help a

family or the sick and hurt or for playing a hymn on the church piano from memory and totally by ear. What wonderful hands.

Lesson Learned

My Mom was no Saint, but close to it in my eyes. She used the resources that God had given her WELL. She didn't complain in difficult times, in fact would often sing "My God How Wonderful Thou Art" no matter what the situation. All the time though, one thing was certain, her hands were always busy doing her calling of being a wife and mother, sister and daughter and friend.

Chapter 14

Hands II

Dad's hands were as opposite from Mom's as they could be. Weathered, worn, calloused, scarred, scratched, and nicked. Those hands had been around.

I sometimes look at my own hands and try to compare them to my memory of his. Yes, I've got a liver spot there, a scar there and a remnant of an injury there, but my hands never had to drive a team of horses, or shovel manure. Nor did they have to empty a boxcar full of coal or pour cement, haul milk, or load a truck of wood. I've never had to pump gas for a living, or sleep out on the open range.

His hands were calloused from his work, even from driving his school bus on unpaved rural roads, which meant holding on to the wheel and letting it slide through his hands as the ruts and craters challenged his handling skills. As much as I tried, I was never able to master his hand-over-hand top center grip of the steering wheel for endless hours of driving. His hands were far from soft and gentle, except when someone was sick, especially someone elderly. Those hands were always willing to help my Mom cater a wedding or some kind of potluck at the church and he'd even help with the dishes and the cleanup.

They were the hands of a working man, hands that could do a lot of things, some of them well, some of them very well, and some of them just OK. When he died his hands had left their mark, but only once on my behind.

Lesson Learned

I don't know if we need to try and live up to our father's accomplishments. Or if we necessarily need to strive to exceed their expectations. I believe what we need to do is use their example of hard work and dedication as a road map for our lives. The only calluses my hands have are from pens and paper but I know that Dad would approve of how I made a living. I know I was fortunate I didn't have to do it in the physically exhausting way that he did.

Chapter 15

Ditches

At some point in my childhood I became fascinated with ditches. Especially those that were full of water. When we finally got a family car in addition to the "bus", I can remember staring out of the side windows of the faded maroon '48 Chevy 4-door watching the deep ditches alongside of Highway 169, wondering what would happen if we were to swerve into one. Would we drown? Who would survive? What would happen to the car? Would we be stuck with the bus again?

There was a ditch between Mrs. Greenfield's house and our little house. One early spring day sister Carol decided she could walk on water (frozen water) and nature decided she couldn't. The ice broke and Carol went in. There she was, face down, looking like she had already drowned. Older sister Margaret came to the rescue! She jumped in, sister Bette ran for help. I don't know what sister Sharon and I did, but from that point on there was a unique closeness between Carol and her life-saving older sister, Margaret.

Another ditch episode initiated in the church parking lot when Sharon, Carol, Don, and some others dared me to run through the ditch at the end of the lot. I must have just watched a WWII film on TV, because I told them I could make it with my BB gun held over my head like some war hero.

I didn't realize until I was in halfway up to my chest (or was it my cheeks?), in ice cold water that my wet winter clothes were weighing me down, and I needed help to get out of there.

Lesson Learned

Make sure that you know your limitations when attempting to cross a ditch that life puts in front of you. If you get in too deep you may need someone you can count on to bail you out.

Chapter 16

Nothing to Do

One would think that growing up in a small Midwest town in the mid-fifty's would make it almost impossible to get in trouble. On the whole we did pretty well, except when, as my Mom would say, "there was a storm brewing".

For whatever reason, Dad's restless Methodist genes that we inherited would surface once in a while, and one or all of us would end up in trouble (usually me, for picking on my sisters). Sharon, was an easy target, because she would predictably react to teasing, and I could usually push Carol's buttons, but she would tell Mom and that would end it right on the spot. Tattletale!

But an easier target was Cousin Rick. I have no idea now why we chose to tease him so unmercifully and continually. Maybe because, as with Sharon, we knew we were guaranteed a reaction. It was especially fun when we stole his bicycle. That is, until Aunt Abbie would call Mom and then it wasn't fun anymore, at least until the next time.

Lesson Learned

You'll always get caught, but sometimes a little mischief really is fun. I still enjoy a good practical joke especially on Cousin Rick (now known as Fred), but now it's always lighthearted and just in jest.

In fact, even after all the hard times I (we) gave him, it was Fred who stayed by sister Sharon's side at the hospital an entire night after my motorcycle accident in 2004 and it's Fred and his wife Marge who continue to call and check up on me. I guess that really is another lesson in "Grace."

Thanks for the forgiveness, Fred!

Chapter 17

The Other Bus

One day, during the mid-fifties, I was spending the day with my older cousin, Ruth Smith (Boggs) at her job in Milaca. She worked at the local Greyhound bus depot which was connected to the local Coke bottling plant.

What an adventure for a 9 year old boy! Watching the machinery process all those bottles, washing them and filling them with Coke. But the big deal for me was seeing all those huge diesel Greyhound buses come in and out of the depot all day long.

For me, it was a dream come true, but for her it was probably a pain to have her younger cousin hanging around. Even so, she surprised me with a gift. It was "the other bus". A metal 8" miniature version of a Greyhound Scenic Cruiser. Wow! I've never forgotten that gift!

For months, perhaps years, "the other bus" made more cross country trips, and went on more family vacations, than the big old yellow '47 Chevy school bus in the front yard ever did; plus it had an imaginary restroom in it!

In reality, it never made it out of the sand box. In 1958, as we were approaching the Iowa border, on our way to California, I suddenly realized that my means of fantasy and escape was still in the sand box. Try as I might, my father could not be persuaded to turn around to retrieve "the other bus" for me.

Thanks to Sister Sharon another "Greyhound Scenic Crusier" was retrived from e-bay in the summer of 2007. Her thoughtfulness will long be remembered.

Lesson Learned

Each of us had a means of escape and fantasy in our childhood. Sometimes it's necessary and sometimes it carries on over in life. Fortunately, I had a great family I didn't really need to escape from. As the years have gone by and I've grown older, I've given thought more than once of asking my sister Carol, who recently moved back to Minnesota, to rent a metal detector and see if she could find what remains of "the other bus" in the sand pile. Small, seemingly unimportant gifts can mean the world to a young child, forever.

Chapter 18

Names

At birth, I was baptized Duane Stirling Smith. As I understand the tale, I was almost dubbed "Alfred" Stirling Smith, until it was pointed out what my initials would be. I know that Stirling is a family name from an Uncle Stirling Van Kleek, carried on by my father, Walter Stirling Smith, and my cousin, Fredrick Stirling Vedders. I was extremely proud and honored when my daughter Rachel named my grandson, Marcus Stirling Smith. Not only did I feel it honored me personally, it honored the family, past, present, and future.

My family apparently has this thing about names. My father's name was Walter, but he was known as "Buck". My Mother was named Janna at birth which became "Ann".

My oldest sister, Margaret, became Peg. Next in line, sister Elizabeth was known as Liz for years and now is known as Bette. Sharon is about the only one who kept her identity. Carol is usually identified as the "baby sister".

I've really never been known as Duane, except to my mother and school teachers. When I was about 6 weeks old my mother decided it was time to show off the wonderful boy- child to her former co-workers at Nelson's department store in Princeton.

Upon gazing at my rotund body, and bald head (not much has changed). I was promptly dubbed "Butch". Not only did it fit the look of my physique, it apparently fit my personality. "Butch" was the only name I was recognized by for the first 18 years of my life.

During my years of service in the Air Force Smith turned into "Smitty", and so it remains today.

Lesson Learned

Names are what we are known by, those names are who our friends call on the phone and write letters to, or send e-mails to. Am I really "Butch", "Smitty", "Duane" or now, my post-career identity, "D. StiRling Smith"? Who am I really? A few syllables uttered by someone's lips, a few letters typed on a page, or a person that reflects my God, my family, my beliefs and my values?

Some years ago, while on a trip to Minneapolis, I stopped by the cemetery in Pease to pay my respects at my parents resting place.

It's not the busiest place in the universe, but as I was leaving an elderly gentleman came up to me, about scared me to death, and said "you must be Walt and Ann's son "Butch!", I would know you anywhere!"

I hadn't been to Pease since I was 21 years old. I had no idea who he was, but I was honored that he remembered me as "Butch", the son of Walt and Ann Smith.

Chapter 19

More Lessons From Other Small Towns

The vast majority of what is written on these pages was written while I was recovering from a near fatal car/motorcycle accident. For over two and one half years I've had time to reflect on my life. Where I've come from, where I am, and where I'm headed; mentally, physically, and also spiritually.

As I've taken this journey, I've been blessed with tremendous support from friends in the "small towns" of my own experience. The "Small Town" of my family molded me in my youth and teenage years. The "Small Town" of my Air Force years taught me the value of loyalty, honor and doing your duty.

The "Small Town" of my College years and early working career years gave me the satisfaction of hard work and focus. The "Small Town" of my church gave me support and encouragement when I was struggling with very personal things.

When my daughter Rachel was tragically killed by a drunk driver, three "Small Towns', my work community, my church and my family continued to uplift me with prayers and acts of kindness and care.

After my near fatal accident my condo neighborhood and church family provided meals, hospital and home visits, transportation, cards and phone calls. That kind of caring continues to this day.

Most importantly, my wife, Janie came to be my wife because we both belong to our church's "Small Town". She thought bringing me a homemade apple pie would make me feel better. She was never so right in her life!

Lesson Learned:

So what am I trying to say? All around us there are opportunities to build relationships. It may be in a large metropolitan area, a rural area, or someplace in-between. It really makes little, if any, difference. What matters is that we build relationships which foster "Small Town" lessons. Lessons that impact people's lives where they live every day. Places where you and I function, where our families live, and where we will die.

I'm grateful that I was fortunate to have grown up in "Small Town" America, and that throughout my life there were people who cared enough to teach me some of life's "Small Town" lessons

Oh, one more thing.... **Pease**

Thank You!

Made in the USA
Charleston, SC
26 May 2015